Sea Turtles

by **Trudi Strain Trueit**

Reading Consultant: Nanci R. Vargus, Ed.D.

Picture Words

 eggs

 fish

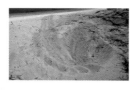 hole

 ocean

 sand

 sea grass

 sea turtle

 sea turtles

 water

What do 🐢🐢 do?

A  swims in the ▮.

A  swims with .

A  sleeps under ●.

A  eats .

A  crawls in .

A  digs a .

A  lays .

Baby swim away!

Words to Know

crawl (KRAWL)
    to move slowly

sea grass (SEE GRASS)
    grass that grows in the ocean

sea turtle (SEE TURT-l)
    a turtle that lives in the ocean and
    has paddles instead of feet

Find Out More

Books

Wearing, Judy. *Sea Turtles*. New York: Weigl Publishing, 2009.

Weber, Valerie J. *Sea Turtles*. Pleasantville, NY: Weekly Reader Books, 2009.

Wilsdon, Christina. *Turtles*. Chicago, IL: Gareth Stevens, 2009.

DVD

Galapagos: Beyond Darwin, Discovery Communications, 2008.

Websites

NOAA Fisheries: Sea Turtles
www.nmfs.noaa.gov/pr/education/turtles.htm
Save the Turtles
www.costaricaturtles.org
Sea World
www.seaworld.org/fun-zone/index.htm

About the Author

Trudi Strain Trueit lives in Everett, WA, near Puget Sound, where she gets to see many different sea creatures. Trudi is the author of more than sixty fiction and nonfiction books for children, including *Sharks* and *Starfish* in the Benchmark Rebus Ocean Life series. She writes fiction, too, including the popular *Secrets of a Lab Rat* series. Visit her website at **www.truditrueit.com**.

About the Reading Consultant

Nanci R. Vargus, Ed.D., wants all children to enjoy reading. She used to teach first grade. Now she works at the University of Indianapolis. Nanci helps young people become teachers. One of her favorite memories is from a visit to Tortuguero, Costa Rica, where she saw a mother sea turtle laying her eggs.

Copyright © 2011 Marshall Cavendish Corporation

Published by Marshall Cavendish Benchmark
An imprint of Marshall Cavendish Corporation

Website: www.marshallcavendish.us

This publication represents the opinions and views of the author based on Trudi Strain Trueit's personal experience, knowledge, and research. The information in this book serves as a general guide only. The author and publisher have used their best efforts in preparing this book and disclaim liability rising directly and indirectly from the use and application of this book.

Other Marshall Cavendish Offices:
Marshall Cavendish International (Asia) Private Limited, 1 New Industrial Road, Singapore 536196 • Marshall Cavendish International (Thailand) Co Ltd. 253 Asoke, 12th Flr, Sukhumvit 21 Road, Klongtoey Nua, Wattana, Bangkok 10110, Thailand • Marshall Cavendish (Malaysia) Sdn Bhd, Times Subang, Lot 46, Subang Hi-Tech Industrial Park, Batu Tiga, 40000 Shah Alam, Selangor Darul Ehsan, Malaysia

Marshall Cavendish is a trademark of Times Publishing Limited

All websites were available and accurate when this book was sent to press.

Library of Congress Cataloging-in-Publication Data
Trueit, Trudi Strain.
Sea turtles / Trudi Strain Trueit.
    p. cm. — (Ocean life)
Includes bibliographical references.
Summary: "A simple introduction to sea turtles using rebuses"—Provided by publisher.
ISBN 978-0-7614-4895-2
1. Sea turtles—Juvenile literature. I. Title.
QL666.C536T78 2009
597.92'8—dc22
2009025473

Editor: Christina Gardeski
Publisher: Michelle Bisson
Art Director: Anahid Hamparian
Series Designer: Virginia Pope

Photo research by Connie Gardner
Cover photo by Paul Souders/*Corbis*

The photographs in this book are used by permission and through the courtesy of: *Peter Arnold*: pp. 5, 15 Reinhard Dirscherl; p. 11 Jonathan Bird; p. 13 Huguet Pierre. *SuperStock*: p. 7 Pacific Stock, p. 19 age fotostock. *Getty Images*: p. 2 Sri Lanka Bentora, eggs; Vikki Hart, fish, Jason Edwards, hole; Tetra Images, ocean; Jodie Coston, sand; p.3 Sami Sarkis, sea grass; Paul Souders, sea turtle; Comstock, water; p. 9 Jeff Hunter. *Corbis*: p. 17 Kevin Schafer. *Art Life Images*: p. 21 age fotostock.

Printed in Malaysia (T)
1 3 5 6 4 2